Report No. SPO-2010-003   June 18, 2010

Inspector General
United States
Department *of* Defense

I0426196

Review of DoD Compliance with

Section 847 of the NDAA for FY 2008

DEPARTMENT OF DEFENSE OFFICE OF INSPECTOR GENERAL

 *Vision: "One professional team strengthening the integrity, efficiency, and effectiveness of Department of Defense programs and operations."*

General Information

Forward questions or comments concerning this assessment and report and other activities conducted by the Office of Special Plans & Operations to:

Office of the Deputy Inspector General
for Special Plans & Operations
Department of Defense Office of Inspector General
400 Army Navy Drive
Arlington, VA 22202-4704
or
E-mail: spo@dodig.mil

An overview of the Office of Special Plans & Operations mission and organization and a list of past evaluations and future topics are available at http://www.dodig.mil.

To Report Fraud, Waste, and Abuse

Contact the Department of Defense Office of Inspector General hotline at (800)424-9098, E-mail at hotline@dodig.mil or write:

Defense Hotline
The Pentagon
Washington, DC 20301-1900

INSPECTOR GENERAL
DEPARTMENT OF DEFENSE
400 ARMY NAVY DRIVE
ARLINGTON, VIRGINIA 22202-4704

JUN 1 8 2010

MEMORANDUM FOR GENERAL COUNSEL OF THE DEPARTMENT OF DEFENSE

SUBJECT: Review of Department of Defense Compliance with Section 847 of the National Defense Authorization Act for Fiscal Year 2008 (Report No. SPO-2010-003)

Section 847 of the National Defense Authorization Act for Fiscal Year 2008 requires a selected category of senior Department of Defense (DoD) acquisition officials to seek a post-employment ethics opinion letter before accepting compensation from a DoD contractor. Section 847 also requires DoD ethics officials issue written opinion letters within 30 days after receiving a request for an opinion and that copies of such opinions are maintained in a centralized database or repository. The DoD Inspector General is required to perform periodic reviews to ensure that written opinions are being provided and retained in accordance with the requirements of the statute.

Consistent with the requirements of Section 847, the DoD Office of Inspector General reviewed the progress of the DoD Standards of Conduct Office (SOCO) in the DoD Office of General Counsel in developing the required centralized database or repository, as well as other actions taken by SOCO to comply with Section 847. The enclosed report provides the results of this review.

Should you have any questions, please contact me at (703) 604-9262 or Mr. J. Philip VanLandingham at (703) 604-8948 or Dr. Sardar Q. Hassan at (703) 604-9146.

Kenneth P. Moorefield
Deputy Inspector General
Special Plans and Operations

Results in Brief: Review of DoD Compliance with Section 847 of the NDAA for FY 2008

What We Did

Section 847 of the National Defense Authorization Act (NDAA) for FY 2008, Public Law 110-181, requires a selected category of senior DoD acquisition officials to seek a post-employment DoD ethics opinion letter before accepting compensation from a DoD contractor. The ethics officials are required to issue the written opinion letter within 30 days after receiving the request. DoD is required to maintain copies of these opinion letters in a centralized database/repository. The Inspector General is required to perform periodic reviews to ensure that written opinions are being provided and retained in accordance with the requirements of this section. Also, defense contractors are required, prior to compensating a former DoD official, to determine that the former DoD official has sought and received (or has not received after 30 days of seeking) a written opinion from the appropriate ethics counselor.

We reviewed the progress of the DoD Standards of Conduct Office (SOCO) in the DoD Office of General Counsel (OGC) in developing the required centralized repository as well as other actions taken by SOCO to promote compliance with the requirements of Section 847. We also reviewed existing procedures in place for receiving requests from covered DoD officials, processing the requests, issuing opinion letters, and storing copies of opinion letters. Additionally, we advised SOCO to issue a data call to gather information about the opinion letters issued by all the Component Ethics offices.

What We Found

As a result of our document reviews and interviews, we found:

- DoD OGC / SOCO has initiated but not completed development and implementation of a central DoD repository to record requests for written opinions and to store copies of opinion letters issued.
- Current procedures for receiving requests and issuing opinion letters are decentralized.
- DoD OGC / SOCO has disseminated information on Section 847 requirements to promote compliance within the DoD and the defense contracting community.

What We Recommend

1. The Standards of Conduct Office in the DoD Office of General Counsel:
   a. continue the development and implementation of a central DoD repository in an expeditious manner in order to meet the statutory requirement.
   b. ensure that all Component Ethics offices are informed regarding SOCO's development of a centralized database application, and their roles and responsibilities for meeting the statutory requirement for a DoD-wide central repository.

2. The Standards of Conduct Office in the DoD Office of General Counsel:
   a. implement procedures to obtain from Component Ethics offices copies of requests for written opinions pursuant to Section 847, as well as each written opinion provided pursuant to such a request, until such time that After Government Employment Advisory Repository (AGEAR) is operational.
   b. ensure that these existing requests for written opinions and copies of written opinions issued are transferred into AGEAR, at such time that AGEAR is operational.

Client Comments and Our Response

The DoD Office of General Counsel concurred with our recommendations and provided the latest status on the progress towards development of the centralized DoD repository. Client comments are included in Appendix C.

Recommendations Table

Client /OPR	Recommendations Requiring Comment	No Additional Comments Required
The Standards of Conduct Office in the DoD Office of General Counsel		1.a, 1.b, 2.a, 2.b

Total Recommendations in this Report: 4

Table of Contents

Introduction

Background

Paragraphs (a)(1) and (a)(2) of Section 847 of the National Defense Authorization Act for FY 2008, Public Law 110-181, requires all "covered DoD officials," as defined in paragraph (c) of Section 847, to obtain a post-employment ethics opinion letter from an appropriate DoD ethics official, if within two years after leaving service in the DoD the covered DoD official expects to receive compensation from a DoD contractor.

Paragraph (a)(3) states:
"WRITTEN OPINION- Not later than 30 days after receiving a request by an official or former official of the Department of Defense described in subsection (c), the appropriate ethics counselor shall provide such official or former official a written opinion regarding the applicability or inapplicability of post-employment restrictions to activities that the official or former official may undertake on behalf of a contractor."

In addition, paragraph (a)(4) prohibits DoD contractors from knowingly providing compensation to a former DoD official within two years after such official leaves service in DoD, without first determining that the former official has sought and received (or has not received after 30 days of seeking) a written opinion from the appropriate ethics counselor regarding the applicability of post-employment restrictions to the activities that the former official is expected to undertake on behalf of the contractor.

Further, Paragraph "(b) Recordkeeping Requirement" of Section 847 describes storage and oversight requirements for the opinion letters as quoted below.

Paragraph (b)(1) DATABASE:
"Each request for a written opinion made pursuant to this section, and each written opinion provided pursuant to such a request, shall be retained by the Department of Defense in a central database or repository for not less than five years beginning on the date on which the written opinion was provided."

Paragraph (b)(2) INSPECTOR GENERAL REVIEW:
"The Inspector General of the Department of Defense shall conduct periodic reviews to ensure that written opinions are being provided and retained in accordance with the requirements of this section. The first such review shall be conducted no later than two years after the date of the enactment of this Act."

On September 26, 2008, the DoD IG team participated in a meeting with representatives from the Standards of Conduct Office (SOCO) in the DoD Office of General Counsel (DoD OGC). Based on the information obtained during the meeting, the DoD IG team developed plans to base this review on the DoD OGC / SOCO central database / repository once it was operational. However, as of November 5, 2009, the centralized database was still in demonstration phase.

Therefore, the DoD IG team decided to also review existing non-centralized procedures and summary data collected from Component Ethics offices.

Objectives

The overall objective of this evaluation was to review the status of DoD compliance with the recordkeeping requirements of Section 847. Specific objectives were to:

- Review the status of central repository development and implementation by the Standards of Conduct Office in the Office of the General Counsel of the Department of Defense.
- Review the existing interim processes to store copies of the opinion letters.
- Review the existing processes through which covered DoD personnel, who are expecting compensation from any DoD contractor(s), request written opinion letters from the appropriate ethics counselor.
- Review the existing processes for providing written opinion letters regarding the applicability of post employment restrictions on activities that the DoD official or former official may undertake on behalf of a contractor.

Methodology

DoD IG team attended three meetings organized by the DoD OGC / SOCO on the following dates – September 26, 2008, February 18, 2009, and November 5, 2009. Subsequently, the DoD IG team developed a detailed project design in December of 2009.

The DoD IG team arranged for a follow up meeting with SOCO representatives on December 18, 2009. The information collected at the December 18, 2009 meeting was responsive and the DoD IG team further requested that SOCO issue a data call to all DoD Component ethics officials for summarized/tabulated data on opinion letters issued to comply with the requirements of Section 847. On January 4, 2010, SOCO issued the data call with a suspense date of January 15, 2010. DoD Component ethics officials provided copies of 219 opinion letters, which SOCO forwarded to the DoD IG Team.

The DoD IG team independently developed a compilation of activities that SOCO had either planned to complete or had already completed to promote compliance with the new requirements. The list of SOCO activities was validated during a meeting with SOCO on February 17, 2010. Subsequent to this meeting, SOCO provided an organized and comprehensive list of completed activities. Significant items from this list are presented in Observation 3. For further discussion of methodology and acronyms used in this report, see Appendix A.

Observations and Recommendations

Observation 1

DoD OGC / SOCO has initiated but not completed development and implementation of a central DoD repository to record requests for written opinions and to store copies of opinion letters issued.

As of April 7, 2010, SOCO had not implemented a centralized database repository that records requests and issuances of opinion letters.

In February 2009, SOCO and the Army OGC, along with the other stakeholders, developed a draft "Requirements Document" for a centralized database, to be referred to as "After Government Employment Advisory Repository" (AGEAR), and provided a copy to all stakeholders. On November 5, 2009, SOCO held a meeting to demonstrate the capabilities of AGEAR's latest test version. As per the AGEAR Project Officer's presentation, AGEAR will have the following capabilities in addition to the ability to store the opinion letters.

1) Enable the requestor to:
   - submit a request for an opinion letter
   - view the status of each request
   - receive notifications from the AGEAR Project Officer / Ethics Official
   - submit additional information
   - receive the actual opinion letter

2) Enable the Ethics Officials from all DoD Component Ethics offices to:
   - review the request for opinion letters
   - instruct the requestor to provide additional information or to complete a questionnaire
   - record all actions they may have taken on the request
   - obtain assistance from other experts
   - prepare and issue the opinion letter to the requestor

When asked about whether usage of the central repository would be mandatory for all Component Ethics offices, the AGEAR Project Officer stated that they had not made any final decision in this regard. It was first proposed that Component Ethics offices would first need to determine the convenience and efficiency of the new DoD-wide centralized repository, and over time, adopt it as the method of choice. DoD IG team communicated to the SOCO representatives that all opinion letters are required by the Section 847 legislation to be in a DoD-wide central repository. Ultimately, SOCO representatives agreed that utilization of the AGEAR application would become a requirement for all Component Ethics offices.

Recommendation 1

We recommend that the Standards of Conduct Office in the DoD Office of General Counsel:

a. continue the development and implementation of a central DoD repository in an expeditious manner in order to meet the statutory requirement.

b. ensure that all Component Ethics offices are informed regarding SOCO's development of a centralized database application, and their roles and responsibilities for meeting the statutory requirement for a DoD-wide central repository.

Observation 2

Current procedures for receiving requests and issuing opinion letters are decentralized.

Presently, any former or current DoD official who needs an opinion letter (to meet the requirements of Section 847) requests the letter from the designated ethics official in the DoD Component for which the official is working or last worked. Each Component Ethics office processes the requests from personnel in their own Component and maintains a record of actions taken, including copies of opinion letters issued.

Component Ethics officials, prior to issuing the opinion letters, require covered DoD personnel to fill out a questionnaire (referenced in the link below). The information obtained is used as the basis for completing the opinion letter.
http://www.dod.mil/dodgc/defense_ethics/resource_library/09_PGSE_Questionnaire.doc (last accessed March 2, 2010).

On January 4, 2010, DoD OGC / SOCO issued a data call requiring all Component Ethics offices to forward to SOCO all opinion letters that were issued as per the requirements of Section 847. As of January 15, 2010, copies of written opinion letters, issued by the Component Ethics offices, were centrally located at SOCO, however this is not yet the established procedure.

Recommendation 2

We recommend that the Standards of Conduct Office in the DoD Office of General Counsel:

(a) implement procedures to obtain from Component Ethics offices copies of requests for written opinions pursuant to Section 847, as well as each written opinion provided pursuant to such a request, until such time that AGEAR is operational.

(b) ensure that these existing requests for written opinions and copies of written opinions issued are transferred into AGEAR, at such time that AGEAR is operational.

Observation 3

DoD OGC / SOCO has disseminated information on the Section 847 requirements to promote compliance within the DoD and the defense contracting community.

The Director of SOCO was personally involved in the following high-visibility dissemination activities:

- presented information on Section 847 at the Defense Industry Initiative on Business Ethics and Conduct, on June 27, 2008.
- participated in briefing all outgoing senior officials as part of the DoD transition.
- briefed the Secretary of Defense in his 2008 annual ethics training on the "revolving door concerns" and the application of Section 847.

In addition, SOCO has:

a. Disseminated information related to Section 847 requirements in three of its 2008 advisories found in the Ethics Resource Library on the SOCO website. (http://www.dod.mil/dodgc/defense_ethics/) (accessed on March 2, 2010)

   The Advisory Numbers are: 08-02 (issued on February 22, 2008), 08-03 (issued on April 28, 2008), and 08-04 (issued on June 12, 2008). Most of the documents listed below are in these three advisories on the SOCO website.

b. Developed a questionnaire for departing DoD personnel that will both (i) inform the departing official about the various ethics requirements (including Section 847 requirements) and (ii) provide data to the ethics offices to identify individuals who may be required to seek ethics opinion before working for certain defense contractors. http://www.dod.mil/dodgc/defense_ethics/resource_library/09_PGSE_Questionnaire.doc (accessed on March 2, 2010)

c. Developed a set of sample legal opinion templates which can be customized by ethics officials to efficiently prepare the ethics advisory. http://www.dod.mil/dodgc/defense_ethics/resource_library/Section_847_Cover_Memo.doc (accessed on March 2, 2010)

d. Amended the model certification required for Public Financial Disclosure report filers by Subsection 8-400 of DoD 5500.7-R, Joint Ethics Regulation, to include Section 847 and placed it on the SOCO website for use throughout the Department. SOCO has amended its post-employment model guidance to include Section 847 notice and has replaced the old guidance on its website.

   SOCO provided us copies of all the certifications used since adoption of the Section 847 requirements - 2008 Annual Postemployment Certification.doc, 2009 Annual

Postemployment Certification.doc, and 2010 Postemployment Certification.doc. However, only the 2009 version was posted on the SOCO website.

e. Issued a change request that resulted in the following amendment to DFARS paragraph 209.406-2 "Causes for Debarment" - new item (2): *"(2) Any contractor that knowingly provides compensation to a former DoD official in violation of Section 847 of the National Defense Authorization Act for Fiscal Year 2008 (Pub. L. 110-181) may face suspension and debarment proceedings in accordance with 41 U.S.C. 423(e)(3)(A)(iii)."*

f. Issued a change request that resulted in modification of SUBPART 203-1 (SAFEGUARDS) of the DFARs. The following items were added in Paragraph 203-171.

"203.171 Senior DoD officials seeking employment with defense contractors.

203.171-1 Scope.
This section implements Section 847 of the National Defense Authorization Act for Fiscal Year 2008 (Pub. L. 110-181).

203.171-2 Definition.
"Covered DoD official," as used in this section, is defined in the clause at 252.203-7000, Requirements Relating to Compensation of Former DoD Officials.

203.171-3 Policy.

(a) A DoD official covered by the requirements of Section 847 of Pub. L. 110-181 (a "covered DoD official") who, within 2 years after leaving DoD service, expects to receive compensation from a DoD contractor, shall, prior to accepting such compensation, request a written opinion from the appropriate DoD ethics counselor regarding the applicability of post-employment restrictions to activities that the official may undertake on behalf of a contractor.

(b) A DoD contractor may not knowingly provide compensation to a covered DoD official within 2 years after the official leaves DoD service unless the contractor first determines that the official has received, or has requested at least 30 days prior to receiving compensation from the contractor, the post-employment ethics opinion described in paragraph (a) of this section.

(c) If a DoD contractor knowingly fails to comply with the requirements of the clause at 252.203-7000, administrative and contractual actions may be taken, including cancellation of a procurement, rescission of a contract, or initiation of suspension or debarment proceedings.

203.171-4 Contract clause.
Use the clause at 252.203-7000, Requirements Relating to Compensation of Former DoD Officials, in all solicitations and contracts."

Appendix A. Methodology and Acronyms

Methodology

DoD Assistant Inspector General for Inspections & Evaluations and the DoD IG Project Manager for this project first met with the representatives from DoD OGC / SOCO in September 2008.

The DoD IG team attended three meetings organized by the DoD OGC / SOCO on the following dates – September 26, 2008, February 18, 2009, and November 5, 2009. Subsequently, the DoD IG team developed a detailed project design in December of 2009.

On December 3, 2009, the DoD IG team initiated efforts to schedule an interview with SOCO representatives to clarify a number of issues previously researched; to discuss responses to questions developed by the DoD IG team; and to gather additional information required to meet the objectives of the project. The questions to be discussed at the interview were provided at the time of the meeting request.

The DoD IG team arranged for a follow up meeting with SOCO representatives on December 18, 2009. The information collected at the December 18, 2009 meeting was responsive and the DoD IG team further requested that SOCO issue a data call to all DoD Component ethics officials for summarized/tabulated data on opinion letters issued to comply with the requirements of Section 847. On January 4, 2010, SOCO issued the data call with a suspense date of January 15, 2010. DoD Component ethics officials provided copies of 219 opinion letters, which SOCO forwarded to the DoD IG Team.

The DoD IG team independently developed a compilation of activities that SOCO had either planned to complete or had already completed to promote compliance with the new requirements. This listing was provided to SOCO for verification of factual accuracy and completeness on January 21, 2010. A revised listing was forwarded on January 27, 2010. The list of SOCO activities was validated during a meeting with SOCO on February 17, 2010. Subsequent to this meeting, SOCO provided an organized and comprehensive list of completed activities. Significant items from this list are presented in Observation 3.

Use of Computer-Processed Data

The DoD IG team did not use any computer-processed data for this project.

Acronyms Used in this Report

The following is a list of the acronyms used in this report.

AGEAR	After Government Employment Advisory Repository
DFARS	Defense Federal Acquisition Regulation Supplement
GAO	Government Accountability Office
IG	Inspector General
NDAA	National Defense Authorization Act
OGC	Office of General Counsel
SOCO	Standards of Conduct Office
SPO	Special Plans and Operations

Appendix B. Summary of Prior Coverage

During the last 5 years, the Government Accountability Office (GAO) has issued the following report regarding post-government employment of former DoD officials by the defense contractors.

GAO-08-485, "DEFENSE CONTRACTING: Post-Government Employment of Former DoD Officials Needs Greater Transparency," May 2008

Appendix C. Client Comments

Office of General Counsel Comments

DEPARTMENT OF DEFENSE
OFFICE OF GENERAL COUNSEL
1600 DEFENSE PENTAGON
WASHINGTON, DC 20301-1600

MAY 2 4 2010

MEMORANDUM FOR DEPUTY INSPECTOR GENERAL FOR SPECIAL PLANS
AND OPERATIONS, OFFICE OF THE INSPECTOR
GENERAL, DEPARTMENT OF DEFENSE

Subject: Review of DoD Compliance with Section 847 of NDAA for FY2008
Project No. D2010-DIP0E2-0105

This memorandum forwards the Office of General Counsel (GC) response to the subject draft audit report. A copy of the response is attached.

The Office of General Counsel appreciates the opportunity to comment on the subject report. For questions or concerns, please contact Eric Rishel. He may be reached at Eric.Rishel@osd.mil or (703) 571-9444.

Robert S. Taylor
Principal Deputy General Counsel

Attachment:
As stated

PROJECT NO. D2010-DIP0E2-0105

Review of DoD Compliance with Section 847 of NDAA for FY2008

DOD OFFICE OF THE GENERAL COUNSEL (GC) COMMENTS TO THE DOD OIG RECOMMENDATIONS.

Recommendation 1

We recommend that the Standards of Conduct Office in the DoD Office of General Counsel:

a. continue the development and implementation of a central DoD repository in an expeditious manner in order to meet the statutory requirement.

> **RESPONSE TO 1.a.:** Concur. The General Counsel has no legal or policy objection to the recommendation. The Standards of Conduct Office (SOCO) is actively pursuing an internet-based platform to receive requests and store opinions. The Army has developed the After Government Employment Advisory Repository (AGEAR) application which received OMB approval on 12 April 2010. The program utilizes the existing Financial Disclosure Management system software suite and similarly allows for electronic submission by clients, sharing among responsible reviewers, and reports for the IG and other oversight officials. After some administrative coordination and minor changes the application began operation for Army personnel on 23 April 2010. The Army Designated Agency Ethics Official issued a policy memorandum directing that all Army ethics officials would use the application to request and prepare Section 847 advice. All Army ethics officials received notice of the requirement. The Army is conducting a 90 day evaluation to review the process and ensure the application is performing as expected. After the evaluation period, DoD SOCO will receive a briefing on the Army's findings and the results of the evaluation. We anticipate using this information to establish the process for DoD-wide implementation sometime in early August 2010.

b. ensure that all Component Ethics offices are informed regarding SOCO's development of a centralized database application, and their roles and responsibilities for meeting the statutory requirement for a DoD-wide central repository.

RESPONSE TO 1.b.: Concur. The General Counsel has no objection to the recommendation. In its initial guidance issued in 2008, SOCO advised all component ethics officials that Section 847 requires the Department to retain each written request and the applicable written opinion for at least five years from the date of the written opinion in a central database or repository. We directed that each DoD component DAEO establish a procedure or mechanism within their agency that permits the timely retrieval of this data for required periodic reviews by the Department of Defense Inspector General. During the successful data call to provide Inspector General review for this report, we reminded each office issuing covered opinions of the reporting and retention requirements.

Recommendation 2

We recommend that the Standards of Conduct Office in the DoD Office of General Counsel:

a. implement procedures to obtain from Component Ethics offices copies of requests for written opinions pursuant to Section 847, as well as each written opinion provided pursuant to such a request, until such time that AGEAR is operational.

RESPONSE TO 2.a.: Concur. The General Counsel has no objection to the recommendation. As the report notes, in DoD, multiple designated agency ethics officials (DAEOs) and at least dozens of DoD entity Deputy DAEOs have separate, independent authority and responsibility to provide and retain ethics advisory opinions. During the data call to provide Inspector General review for this report, we directed each office issuing covered Section 847 opinions to forward copies to SOCO to allow for IG review. The retention collection requirement is reiterated in SOCO publications, including regular advisories posted to the SOCO website and the annual Ethics Deskbook. Upon full implementation of AGEAR, SOCO will be able to electronically compile and retrieve requests for opinions and issued written ethics advisory memoranda.

b. ensure that these existing requests for written opinions and copies of written opinions issued are transferred into AGEAR, at such time that AGEAR is operational.

RESPONSE TO 2.b.: Concur. The General Counsel has no legal or policy objection to the recommendation. We are working closely with the appropriate information technology experts to fashion a viable mechanism for transferring and retaining this information upon completion of the AGEAR operational test and rollout described above.

ii

Appendix D. Report Distribution

Office of the Secretary of Defense

General Counsel*

Department of the Army

Inspector General, Department of the Army

Department of the Navy

Naval Inspector General

Department of the Air Force

Inspector General, Department of the Air Force

Congressional Committees

Senate Subcommittee on Defense, Committee on Appropriations
Senate Committee on Armed Services
Senate Committee on Homeland Security and Governmental Affairs
House Subcommittee on Defense, Committee on Appropriations
House Committee on Armed Services
House Committee on Homeland Security and Governmental Affairs

* Recipient of the draft report